contents

Key

Number and Place value

Addition and Subtraction

Multiplication and Division

Shape and Measure

Fractions

Mixed Operations

How to use this book

The first page of each section will have a title telling you what the next few pages are about.

Your teacher may tell you to GRAB something that might help you answer the questions.

Sometimes a character will give you a tip.

Read the instructions carefully before each set of questions.

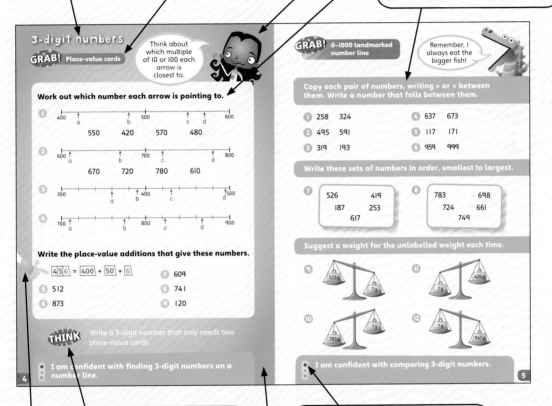

THINK questions will challenge you to think more about the maths on the page.

Choose a traffic light colour to say how confident you are with the maths on the page.

Some pages will show you an example or model.

Each area of maths has its own colour.

3-digit numbers

GRAB! Place-value cards

Think about which multiple of 10 or 100 each arrow is closest to.

Work out which number each arrow is pointing to.

1

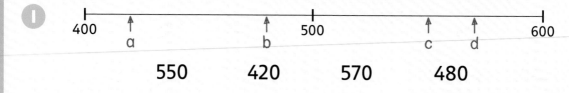

400 ↑a   ↑b 500   ↑c ↑d 600

550   420   570   480

2

400 ↑a   ↑b   700 ↑c   ↑d 800
600

670   720   780   610

3

300   ↑a ↑b 400   ↑c   ↑d 500

4

700 ↑a   ↑b 800   ↑c   ↑d 900

Write the place-value additions that give these numbers.

456 = 400 + 50 + 6

5 512

6 873

7 609

8 741

9 120

THINK Write a 3-digit number that only needs two place-value cards.

○ **I am confident with finding 3-digit numbers on a**
○ **number line.**
○

Remember, I always eat the bigger fish!

Copy each pair of numbers, writing > or < between them. Write a number that falls between them.

1. 258   324

2. 495   591

3. 319   193

4. 637   673

5. 117   171

6. 959   999

Write these sets of numbers in order, smallest to largest.

7.
526		419
187		253
	617	

8.
783		698
724		661
	749	

Suggest a weight for the unlabelled weight each time.

9.
573 g   ? g

11.
? g   426 g

10.
783 g   ? g

12.
? g   947 g

○ **I am confident with comparing 3-digit numbers.**

Write the runners' numbers in order, smallest to largest.

1 539 509 499 555 517 513

2 198 168 177 291 223 286

Write these runners' numbers in order, largest to smallest.

3 719 679 707 682 741 738

4 464 469 481 418 452 490

Suggest a number for each missing value.

There are lots of right answers to these!

5 400 + 40 + 3 < 400 + ☐ + 1

6 800 + 70 + 1 > ☐ + 80 + 5

7 600 + 20 + 7 > 600 + ☐ + 9

8 ☐ + 90 + 4 < 500 + 80 + 6

9 700 + ☐ + 2 > 700 + 70 + 5

10 900 + 90 + ☐ < 900 + 90 + 3

 **THINK** Write three place-value additions to make the below true.

☐ + ☐ + ☐ < ☐ + ☐ + ☐ < ☐ + ☐ + ☐

● I am confident with comparing 3-digit numbers.

Solve these problems.

1 A baby hedgehog weighed 110 g when he was born. After 6 weeks he had gained 100 g. How much did it weigh after 6 weeks?

2 Two hedgehogs were brought to the sanctuary. One weighed 275 g and the other weighed 30 g less. How much did the lighter one weigh?

3 A hedgehog weighed 372 g when he arrived at the sanctuary. In the first week he gained 20 g and in the second he gained 105 g. How much did he weigh now?

4 The retail price of a ski jacket was £295. In a sale the price was reduced by £70. How much does the jacket cost now?

5 Some speakers cost £162 to buy online plus a delivery charge of £7. How much is this in total?

6 A TV costs £415 to buy online. In a shop on the High Street the same TV costs £70 more. How much does it cost in the shop?

7 Kim scores 523 points in round one of a computer game. She scores 60 points more in round two. How many points did she score in round two?

8 In a computer game Jo scored 40 points less than Jake. If Jake scored 794 points, how many did Jo score?

9 Rani, Jasmin and Lucas were playing the computer game *World of Wizardry*. Jasmin scored 375 points, Lucas scored 200 points more than Jasmin and Rani scored 30 points less than Lucas. What were Lucas' and Rani's scores?

● I am confident with solving place-value word problems.

Solve these problems.

1. Mel makes a cocktail using 500 ml of orange juice, 80 ml of blackcurrant juice and 105 ml of pineapple juice. How many millilitres of cocktail does she make?

2. Two jugs contain some water. In the first jug there is 462 ml of water. In the second jug there is 35 ml more. How much water is in the second jug?

3. A glass jar holds 536 ml of milk. James pours 60 ml of the milk in the jar into a bowl. How much milk is in the jar now?

4. A shop increases the price of a TV by £70. The TV cost £362 before the price rise. What does it cost now?

5. An mp4 player costs £162 to buy online. It costs £43 more than this to buy it in the shop. How much does it cost in the shop?

6. A bicycle has been reduced by £250 in a sale. It cost £835 before the sale. How much does it cost now?

7. There were 783 adults at a concert. 305 of the adults were women. How many were men?

8. At a football match there were 140 children, 207 women and 342 men. How many were there altogether?

9. On Monday 320 skaters visited an ice rink. On Tuesday there were 208 more skaters at the rink. How many skaters were there on Monday and Tuesday in total?

THINK Write a word problem to go with the addition 460 + 50.

I am confident with solving place-value word problems.

Multiplying and dividing by 10

 $34 \times 10 = 340$

100s	10s	1s
	3	4
3	4	0

Copy and complete these multiplications and divisions.

1 $47 \times 10 = \square$

2 $31 \times 10 = \square$

3 $29 \times 10 = \square$

4 $18 \times 10 = \square$

5 $53 \times 10 = \square$

6 $62 \times 10 = \square$

7 $25 \times 10 = \square$

8 $76 \times 10 = \square$

9 $80 \times 10 = \square$

 $730 \div 10 = 73$

100s	10s	1s
7	3	0
	7	3

10 $140 \div 10 = \square$

11 $310 \div 10 = \square$

12 $290 \div 10 = \square$

13 $360 \div 10 = \square$

14 $790 \div 10 = \square$

15 $830 \div 10 = \square$

16 $250 \div 10 = \square$

17 $500 \div 10 = \square$

18 $990 \div 10 = \square$

 **THINK** What happens to the digits in a number when you make it 10 times bigger? What if you make it 10 times smaller?

● ○ ○ **I am confident with multiplying and dividing by 10.**

Investigation

1   Help me count in 10s from 4 to get to 1004.

2   Help me count in 50s from 4 to get to 1004.

3   Help me count in 100s from 4 to get to 1004.

4   Look at your answers to questions 1, 2 and 3. Which numbers appear in all three counts?

5   What do you notice about the numbers that appear in all three counts?

6   How many more numbers have you written when counting in 50s than when counting in 100s?

7   How many more numbers have you written when counting in 10s than when counting in 100s?

8   Sketch a number line from 0 to 110. Draw arcs to show jumping in 10s from 4 to 104 and to show jumping in 50s from 4 to 104 and to show jumping in 100s from 4 to 104.

 **THINK**   Write a 3-digit number that only needs two place-value cards.

○ **I am confident with counting in 10s, 50s and 100s.**
○
○

Add using partitioning

Answer these additions using partitioning.

① 24 + 57 = ☐

② 71 + 29 = ☐

③ 35 + 47 = ☐

④ 63 + 28 = ☐

⑤ 77 + 18 = ☐

⑥ 62 + 19 = ☐

⑦ 84 + 45 = ☐

⑧ 63 + 72 = ☐

⑨ 32 + 76 = ☐

⑩ 98 + 61 = ☐

⑪ 56 + 63 = ☐

⑫ 83 + 74 = ☐

⑬ 59 + 76 = ☐

⑭ 83 + 77 = ☐

⑮ 65 + 76 = ☐

⑯ 47 + 95 = ☐

⑰ 87 + 47 = ☐

⑱ 93 + 78 = ☐

⑲ 322 + 236 = ☐

⑳ 255 + 423 = ☐

㉑ 583 + 204 = ☐

㉒ 537 + 462 = ☐

Solve these problems.

㉓ One morning a lorry driver drove 63 km. After lunch he drove 19 km further than he had in the morning. How far did he drive altogether that day?

㉔ Amy is 76 cm tall. Ben is 17 cm taller than Amy. Carl is 48 cm taller than Ben. How tall is Carl?

○
○ **I am confident with adding two numbers using**
○ **partitioning.**

1 Write and complete four different 2-digit + 2-digit additions using only these four numbers. Use partitioning.

| 72 | 37 | 85 | 46 |

Answer these additions using partitioning.

2 32 + 39 + 25 = ☐

3 21 + 17 + 38 = ☐

4 26 + 19 + 27 = ☐

5 18 + 27 + 34 = ☐

6 26 + 35 + 17 = ☐

7 28 + 27 + 29 = ☐

8 72 + 33 + 51 = ☐

9 42 + 32 + 75 = ☐

10 48 + 71 + 60 = ☐

11 53 + 62 + 94 = ☐

Now try these.

12 435 + 236 = ☐

13 664 + 228 = ☐

14 755 + 208 = ☐

15 678 + 212 = ☐

Solve these problems.

16 A class conduct a survey, counting the number of vehicles driving past the school. There were 53 cars, 25 vans and 18 motorbikes. How many vehicles altogether?

17 Andy is 68 cm tall. Baz is 27 cm taller than Andy. Carl is 26 cm taller than Baz. How tall is Carl?

I am confident with adding two or three numbers using partitioning.

sorting multiples

Copy and complete the Venn diagram. Write the given numbers into the correct sections.

1

Multiples of 4   Multiples of 5

25, 16, 45, 28, 24, 20, 36, 55, 40, 32, 35

 **THINK** Choose a number that is not a multiple of 4 or 5 and write it in the diagram.

2

Multiples of 2   Multiples of 4

18, 16, 22, 10, 24, 20, 14, 8, 6, 12, 2

 **THINK** Choose a number that is not a multiple of 2 or 4 and write it in the diagram. What is special about the number?

True or false?

3 All multiples of 5 are multiples of 10.

4 All multiples of 4 are even numbers.

5 Every other multiple of 2 is a multiple of 4.

● ○ ○ ○ **I am confident with the 2, 4, 5 and 10 times-tables and recognising links between them.**

Each boat in a race has 8 rowers.
Write the number of rowers in each race.

1

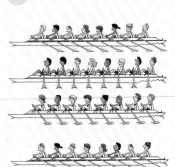

2

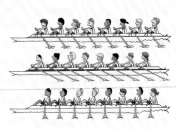

3

4 6 boats

5 8 boats

6 7 boats

Complete the multiplication facts.

7 ☐ × 8 = 24

10 5 × ☐ = 40

13 ☐ × 8 = 72

8 10 × ☐ = 80

11 ☐ × 8 = 56

14 ☐ × 8 = 48

9 ☐ × 8 = 32

12 8 × ☐ = 64

15 ☐ × 8 = 96

Find the missing numbers.

16 ☐ boats will need 16 rowers.

17 12 boats will need ☐ rowers.

18 ☐ boats will need 88 rowers.

19 8 boats will need ☐ rowers.

● **I am confident with the 8 times-table.**
●
●

Write the position of the arrow on each counting stick.

48

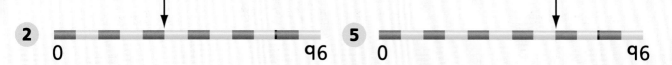

0   96   **3**   0   96

1   0   96   **4**    0   96

2    0   96   **5**   0   96

The children hold up one finger for each 8.
Write how many they have counted.

6

8

10

7

9

11

THINK   How many fingers show multiples of 10?
How many hands are needed to show 240?

Copy and complete these.

12   12 × 8 = ☐   **15**   64 ÷ 8 = ☐   **18**   0 × 8 = ☐

13   5 × 8 = ☐   **16**   6 × 8 = ☐   **19**   24 ÷ 8 = ☐

14   11 × 8 = ☐   **17**   9 × 8 = ☐   **20**   20 × 8 = ☐

●   **I am confident with the 8 times-table.**

Find $\frac{1}{2}$ and then $\frac{1}{4}$ of:

1 8 grapes
2 44 coins
3 £12
4 20p
5 32 tomatoes

6 40 flowers
7 24 sweets
8 80 counters
9 100 g of flour

To find $\frac{1}{4}$ of something, halve and halve again.

When you double and double again you multiply by 4.

Solve these problems.

10 48 playing cards are shared between 2 people. How many do they each get?

11 Could 48 cards be equally shared between 4 people?

12 50 grapes are shared between 2 people. How many do they each get?

13 Could 50 grapes be equally shared between 4 people?

In a computer game points are doubled if you land on a mushroom. Write the new scores.

14 36 → 🍄 = ☐

15 75 → 🍄 = ☐

16 45 → 🍄 → 🍄 = ☐

17 22 → 🍄 → 🍄 = ☐

18 75 → 🍄 → 🍄 = ☐

19 64 → 🍄 → 🍄 = ☐

● I am confident with multiplying and dividing by 4
by doubling or halving twice.

Double each number, double the answer and then double the answer again.

1. 7 → double → double → double

2. 9 → double → double → double

3. 8 → double → double → double

4. 12 → double → double → double

5. 15 → double → double → double

6. 18 → double → double → double

7. Look at your answers. By what number could you have multiplied to get the same answers?

Halve each number, halve the answer and then halve the answer again.

8. 80 → halve → halve → halve

9. 48 → halve → halve → halve

10. 64 → halve → halve → halve

11. 88 → halve → halve → halve

12. 56 → halve → halve → halve

13. Look at your answers. By what number could you have divided to get the same answers?

 You double the 4 times-table to get the 8 times-table. What would you have to do to the 2 times-table to get the 8 times-table?

● I am confident with multiplying and dividing by 8
○ by doubling or halving three times.

Copy each grid and colour the fraction shown.
Then write the fraction of each grid that is not coloured.

1 $\frac{5}{6}$

4 $\frac{5}{9}$

7 $\frac{7}{10}$

2 $\frac{3}{4}$

5 $\frac{2}{5}$

8 $\frac{3}{6}$

3 $\frac{5}{8}$

6 $\frac{2}{3}$

9 $\frac{3}{8}$

THINK Work with a partner. Take turns to say a fraction, e.g. $\frac{5}{8}$.
Your partner says the fraction to make a whole, e.g. $\frac{3}{8}$.

Write what fraction of this group of doors:

10 is red

11 is black

12 has a letter box

13 has a peep-hole

14 has a knocker

15 has a number more than 5

16 has a number less than 7

17 has an odd number

18 has an even number.

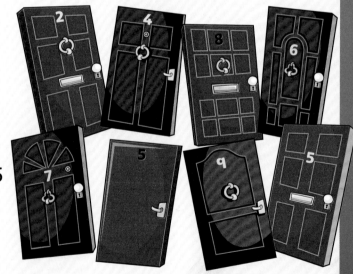

● **I am confident with identifying fractions of an amount.**

1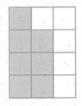

3

5

7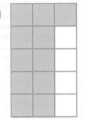

2

4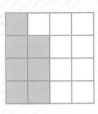

6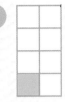

8

Copy and complete each addition to make one whole.

9 $\dfrac{5}{8} + \dfrac{\square}{8} = 1$

14 $\dfrac{\square}{4} + \dfrac{3}{4} = 1$

10 $\dfrac{\square}{6} + \dfrac{4}{6} = 1$

15 $\dfrac{2}{3} + \dfrac{\square}{3} = 1$

11 $\dfrac{3}{9} + \dfrac{\square}{9} = 1$

16 $\dfrac{1}{8} + \dfrac{7}{\square} = 1$

12 $\dfrac{\square}{5} + \dfrac{2}{5} = 1$

17 $\dfrac{\square}{10} + \dfrac{1}{10} = 1$

13 $\dfrac{\square}{10} + \dfrac{4}{\square} = 1$

18 $\dfrac{\square}{5} + \dfrac{4}{\square} = 1$

THINK Write six fractions that are equal to 1.
Write an addition for each.

● ○ ○ ○ **I am confident with identifying fractions of an array and adding to a fraction to make a whole 1.**

Tom Sarah Amal

Jannie Keelin

1. What fraction is one slice of each child's pizza?

2. Keelin eats one slice of her pizza and Tom eats two of his slices. Does Keelin eat more, less or the same amount as Tom?

3. Amal eats two slices of his pizza. What fraction of the pizza does he eat? Does he eat more than half or less than half of his pizza?

4. Tom and Jannie eat the same amount of their pizza. Tom eats $\frac{2}{4}$ of his so how much does Jannie eat?

5. Amal and Sarah eat the same amount of their pizza. Amal eats $\frac{2}{3}$ of his so how much does Sarah eat?

6. What fraction is two slices of each child's pizza?

THINK Write the fraction for each child's whole pizza.

I am confident with identifying fractions of an amount.

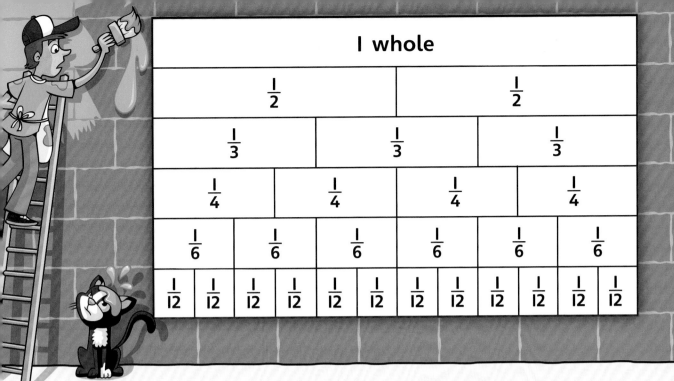

I whole											
$\frac{1}{2}$						$\frac{1}{2}$					
$\frac{1}{3}$				$\frac{1}{3}$				$\frac{1}{3}$			
$\frac{1}{4}$			$\frac{1}{4}$			$\frac{1}{4}$			$\frac{1}{4}$		
$\frac{1}{6}$		$\frac{1}{6}$		$\frac{1}{6}$		$\frac{1}{6}$		$\frac{1}{6}$		$\frac{1}{6}$	
$\frac{1}{12}$	$\frac{1}{12}$	$\frac{1}{12}$	$\frac{1}{12}$	$\frac{1}{12}$	$\frac{1}{12}$	$\frac{1}{12}$	$\frac{1}{12}$	$\frac{1}{12}$	$\frac{1}{12}$	$\frac{1}{12}$	$\frac{1}{12}$

Copy and write the missing numbers.

1. $\frac{1}{2} = \frac{\square}{4}$

2. $\frac{1}{3} = \frac{\square}{6}$

3. $\frac{2}{3} = \frac{\square}{6}$

4. $\frac{6}{6} = \frac{\square}{3}$

5. $\frac{1}{2} = \frac{3}{\square}$

6. $\frac{3}{4} = \frac{\square}{12}$

7. $\frac{3}{12} = \frac{1}{\square}$

8. $\frac{4}{12} = \frac{1}{\square}$

9. $\frac{8}{12} = \frac{\square}{3}$

Answer these questions.

10. Annie cycles 5 km on a 10 km track.
    Ben cycles 15 km along a track of 25 km.
    Ben has cycled more of his track than
    Annie has of her track – true or false?

11. Mena has to give away 3 out of 6 marbles.
    Becky has to give away 4 out of her 8 marbles.
    Are they giving away the same fraction?

I am confident with comparing fractions and finding fraction equivalents.

Write what fraction of each shape is shaded. Then copy the matching number line and mark on the fraction.

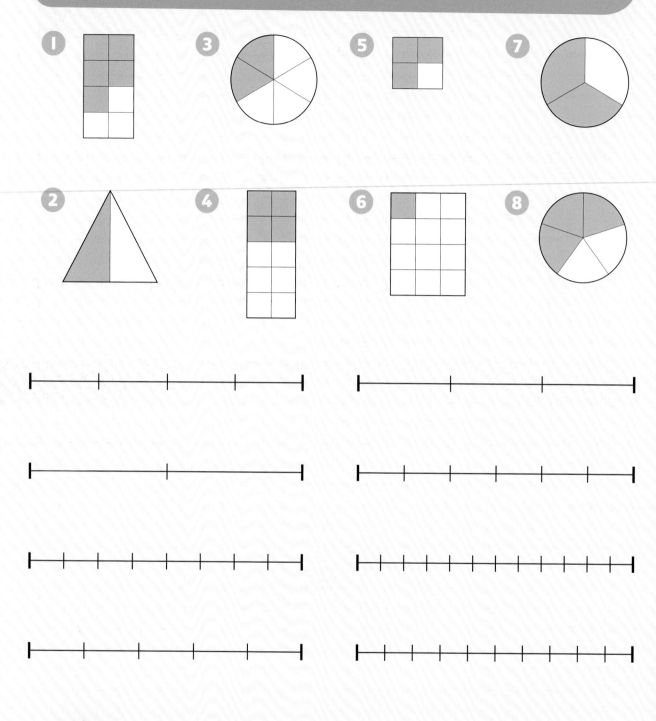

 I am confident with identifying fractions and marking them on a number line.

Write the fraction shown by each arrow.

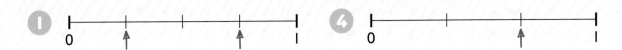

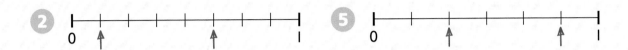

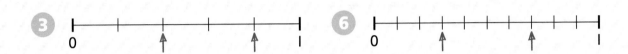

Estimate the fractions marked by these arrows.

 Draw a line with equal divisions. Put an arrow on it and ask your partner to say the fraction. Take turns drawing and answering.

I am confident with identifying fractions on a number line.

Write the fraction shown by each arrow.

1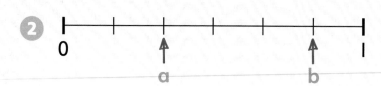

2

3

4

5 Draw your own 0–1 line. Mark it in eighths and label $\frac{3}{8}$ and $\frac{7}{8}$.

6 Draw your own 0–2 line. Mark it in thirds and label $\frac{2}{3}$ and $1\frac{1}{3}$.

7 Draw your own 0–2 line. Mark it in fifths and label $\frac{2}{5}$ and $1\frac{3}{5}$.

THINK Draw a 0–1 line. If you were to mark it in thirds and sixths, which fractions would share the same mark?

 I am confident with identifying and placing fractions on a number line.

Finding fractions of amounts

$\frac{1}{2}$ of 6 = 3

Find these amounts.

① $\frac{1}{3}$ of 6 ② $\frac{2}{3}$ of 6 ③ $\frac{3}{3}$ of 6

④ $\frac{2}{4}$ of 12 ⑥ $\frac{1}{3}$ of 12

⑤ $\frac{3}{4}$ of 12 ⑦ $\frac{2}{3}$ of 12

⑧ $\frac{2}{4}$ of 8 ⑩ $\frac{1}{2}$ of 8

⑨ $\frac{3}{4}$ of 8 ⑪ $\frac{2}{2}$ of 8

○ **I am confident with finding fractions of amounts.**
○
○

Find these amounts.

1 $\frac{1}{3}$ of 6

2 $\frac{2}{3}$ of 6

3 $\frac{3}{3}$ of 6

4 $\frac{1}{3}$ of 15

5 $\frac{2}{3}$ of 15

6 $\frac{3}{3}$ of 15

7 $\frac{1}{5}$ of 15

8 $\frac{2}{5}$ of 15

9 $\frac{4}{5}$ of 15

10 $\frac{1}{4}$ of 20

11 $\frac{3}{4}$ of 20

12 $\frac{4}{4}$ of 20

13 $\frac{1}{5}$ of 20

14 $\frac{3}{5}$ of 20

15 $\frac{4}{5}$ of 20

Copy and complete.

16 $\frac{3}{4}$ of 8

17 $\frac{3}{5}$ of 15

18 $\frac{7}{10}$ of 20

19 $\frac{3}{5}$ of 10

20 $\frac{2}{3}$ of 9

21 $\frac{3}{8}$ of 16

22 $\frac{3}{10}$ of 30

23 $\frac{2}{5}$ of 25

24 $\frac{3}{4}$ of 12

I am confident with finding fractions of amounts.

Recognising angles

Use a right angle measure.

Write which of these angles are right angles.

THINK   Draw a picture with lots of right angles in it.

○ **I am confident with recognising and measuring right angles.**

 **THINK** Use a ruler to draw a right angle, an angle less than 90° and an angle that is more than 90°.

I am confident with recognising, measuring and drawing angles.

Measure the angles in each shape using your right angle measure.

1. List the shapes that have just one right angle.
2. List the shapes that have two right angles.
3. List the shapes that have all right angles.
4. List the shapes that have no right angles.

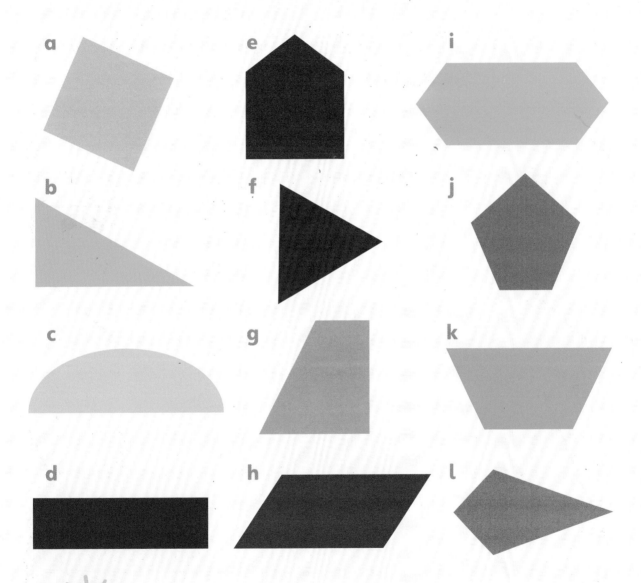

 Draw an irregular shape with two right angles.

Properties of 2D Shapes

Label each shape with its correct name.

hexagon   **pentagon**   **triangle**   **quadrilateral**

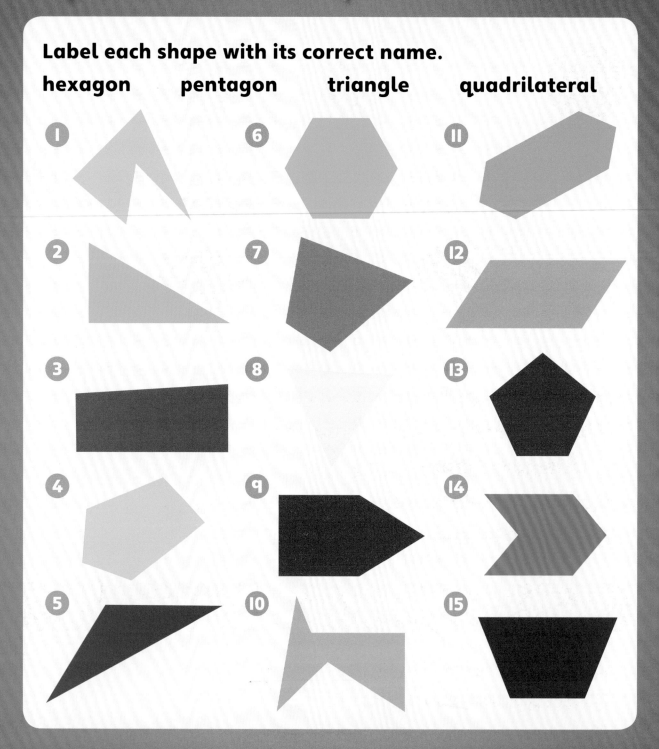

1

2

3

4

5

6

7

8

9

10

11

12

13

14

15

 THINK   Draw as many different looking hexagons as you can draw.

○ **I am confident with recognising triangles,**
quadrilaterals, pentagons and hexagons.

Look at the shapes and answer the questions.

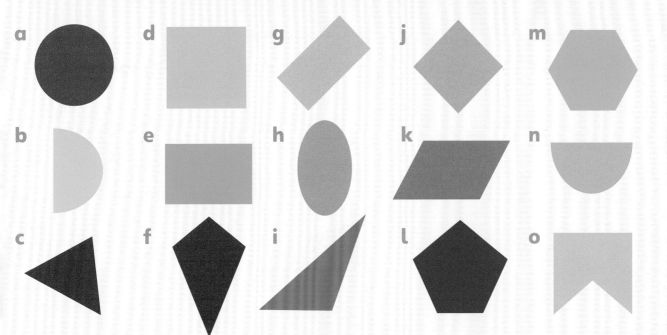

1. List all the quadrilaterals on the page.
2. List all the triangles on the page.
3. List all the circles on the page.
4. List all the rectangles on the page.
5. List all the polygons on the page.

True or false? Discuss with a partner.

6. All rectangles are squares.
7. All squares are rectangles.
8. All rectangles are quadrilaterals.
9. A semi-circle is a polygon.
10. All quadrilaterals are polygons.

I am confident with the properties of 2D shapes.

Look at the shapes and answer the questions.

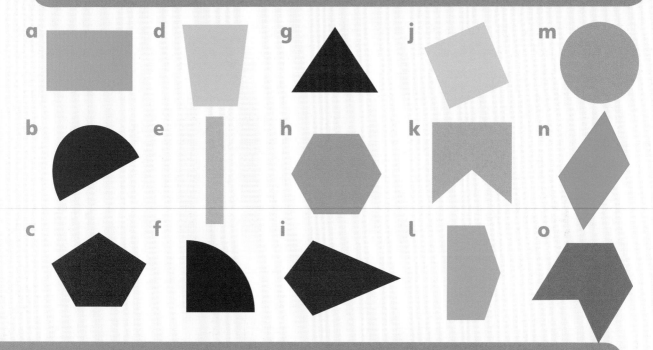

Write which shapes are:

1. quadrilaterals but not rectangles.
2. not polygons.
3. not triangles or quadrilaterals.
4. polygons but not quadrilaterals.
5. polygons but not pentagons or hexagons.

Which of these are always, sometimes or never true?

6. A rectangle is a square.
7. A square is a quadrilateral.
8. A polygon is a triangle.
9. A circle is a polygon.
10. A pentagon is a polygon.

I am confident with the properties of 2D shapes.

Perimeter

How many centimetres would Andy Ant have to walk to find the perimeter of each shape?

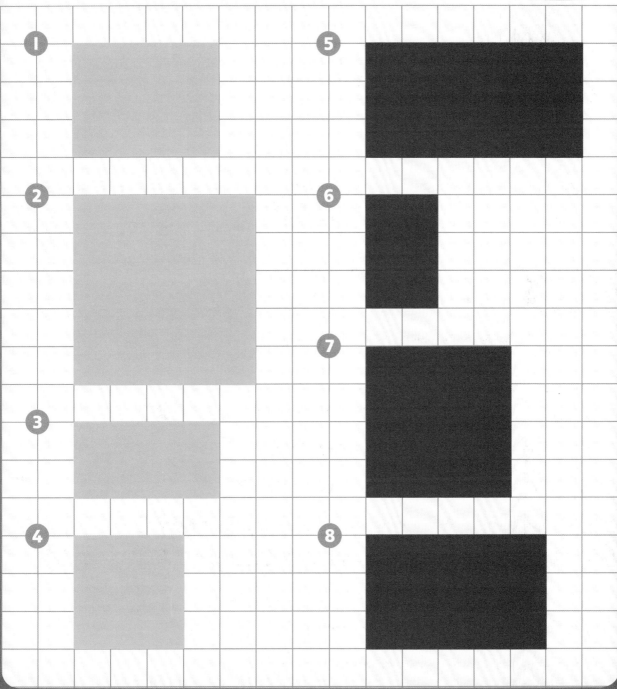

1

2

3

4

5

6

7

8

 **THINK**   Draw a rectangle with a perimeter of 16 cm.

○ ● I am confident with finding the perimeter
○ ○ of different kinds of rectangles.

How many centimetres would Andy Ant have to walk to find the perimeter of each shape?

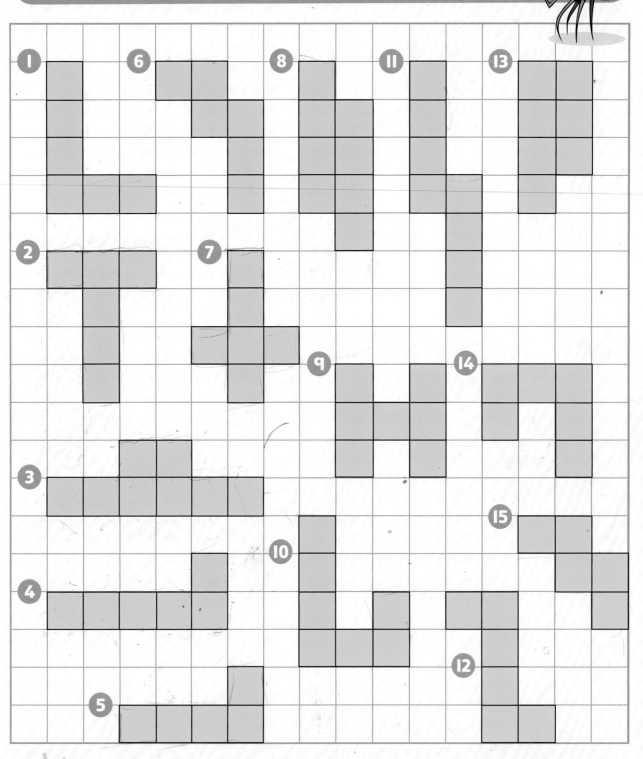

 Draw an 'L' shape of your own with a perimeter of 20 cm.

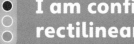 I am confident with finding the perimeter of rectilinear shapes.

Susie the slug is very slow. How many sides of a rectangle does she **have** to crawl around to work out the perimeter?

I am confident with finding the perimeter of regular and irregular polygons.

Use a ruler to measure the perimeter of each shape.

Do you need to measure all five sides?

Write the perimeter of a:

9 rectangle with a length of 10 cm and a side of 7 cm.

10 regular hexagon with a side of 4 cm.

11 square with a side of 11 cm.

THINK Write a rule to work out the perimeter of regular shapes.

○ I am confident with finding the perimeter of regular
○ and irregular polygons.

Relating angles and turns

Through how many degrees does the hand on a clock turn if it moves clockwise:

1 from 12 to 3?

5 from 5 to 8?

2 from 3 to 9?

6 from 4 to 10?

3 from 9 to 12?

7 from 12 to 9?

4 from 1 to 7?

8 from 1 to 4?

Write which number on the clock the hand would point to if it turns clockwise through each given angle.

9 The hand starts at 5 and turns 90°.

10 The hand starts at 2 and turns 180°.

11 The hand starts at 11 and turns 90°.

12 The hand starts at 6 and turns 180°.

13 The hand starts at 8 and turns 90°.

14 The hand starts at 10 and turns 270°.

THINK How many start and end positions are there on a clock face where you can turn through 90°? For example, 12 to 3, 1 to 4 and so on.

○ **I am confident with the relationship between degree turns and angles.**

Place Value and rounding on a number line

The arrows on this line show the numbers 538, 562 and 585.

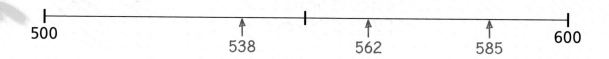

1. Draw a number line from 400 to 500. Mark on the numbers 458, 431 and 409.

2. Draw a number line from 700 to 800. Mark on the numbers 725, 746 and 793.

3. Draw a number line from 200 to 300. Mark on the numbers 281, 264 and 207.

4. Draw a number line from 600 to 700. Mark on the numbers 668, 614 and 688.

5. Draw a number line from 800 to 900. Mark on the numbers 828, 894 and 867.

6. Estimate the number each arrow is pointing to on this line.

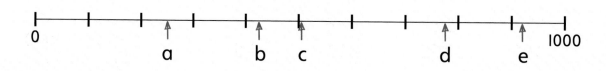

THINK Choose 3 numbers. Round them to the nearest 10, then the nearest 100. Can you find all the 3-digit numbers on the page that round to 500?

● I am confident with placing 3-digit numbers on
○ number lines.
○

Estimate the number for each tag.

Think about where 250, 500 and 750 are.

1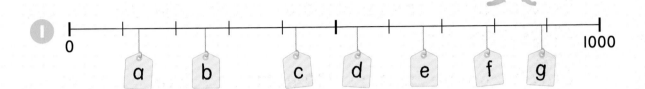
0   a   b   c   d   e   f   g   1000

2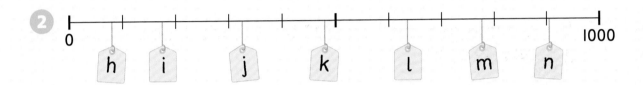
0   h   i   j   k   l   m   n   1000

3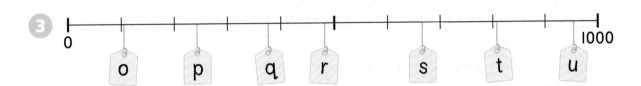
0   o   p   q   r   s   t   u   1000

4 Which of these numbers could this tag be and which could it not? Write yes or no for each number.

637   862   896   740

905   858   823   866

v   1000

 **THINK** Draw a 0–1000 number line and mark a number on it. Get a partner to ask questions to find your number. For example, is your number more than 500? Swap over and do the same again.

I am confident with placing numbers on a 0–1000 number line.

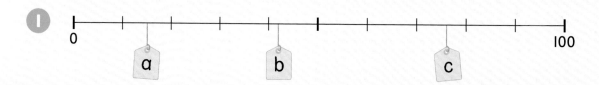

1

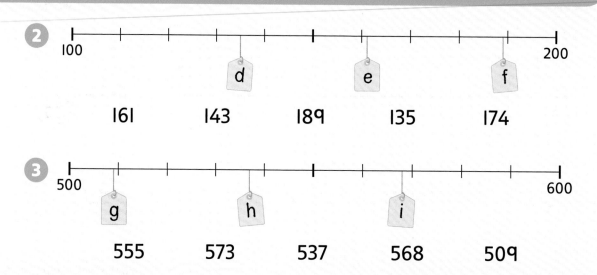

Match the correct number to each tag.
Then round each to the nearest 10.

2

| 161 | 143 | 189 | 135 | 174 |

3

| 555 | 573 | 537 | 568 | 509 |

Match the correct number to each tag.
Then round each to the nearest 100.

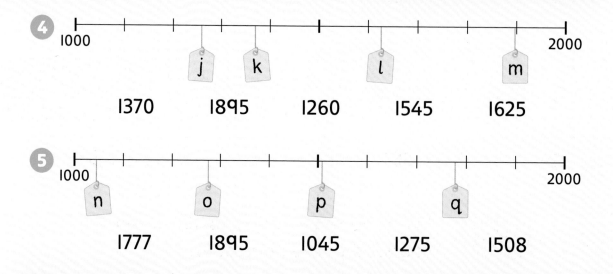

4

| 1370 | 1895 | 1260 | 1545 | 1625 |

5

| 1777 | 1895 | 1045 | 1275 | 1508 |

● ○ ○ ○ **I am confident with placing numbers on a number line and rounding to the nearest 10 or 100.**

For each number draw a number line from the previous 10 to the next 10 and ring the nearest 10. Then draw another line for each number from the previous 100 to the next 100 and ring the nearest 100.

472

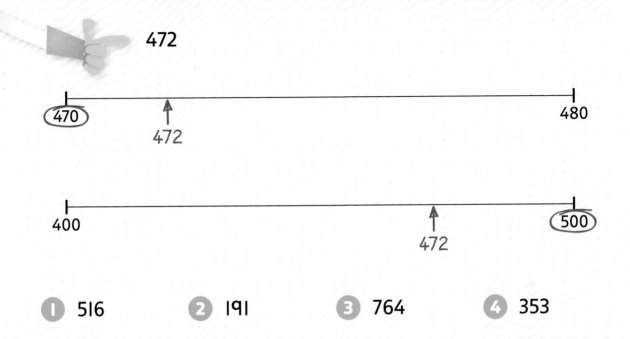

① 516　　　② 191　　　③ 764　　　④ 353

Round these numbers to the nearest 10.
Write how much you have to round up or down by.

⑤ 684　　　⑥ 726　　　⑦ 572　　　⑧ 161

Round these numbers to the nearest 100.
Write how much you have to round up or down by.

⑨ 314　　　⑩ 887　　　⑪ 757　　　⑫ 245

THINK What numbers round to 300 when rounded to the nearest 10?

I am confident with placing numbers on a number line and rounding to the nearest 10 and 100.

Subtract amounts of money by counting up

**You pay £2 for each toy.
How much change will you get for each one?**

20p

Use coins or Frog on a
money line like this.

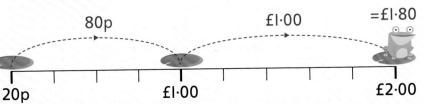

80p   £1·00   =£1·80

20p   £1·00   £2·00

1   40p

3   10p

5   50p

2   70p

4   80p

6   £0·60

THINK   I got £1·50 change when buying a toy motorbike with £2. How much was the toy motorbike?

○ **I am confident with subtracting from £2 by counting up.**
○
○

42

You pay £5 for each of these monsters. How much change will you get for each one?

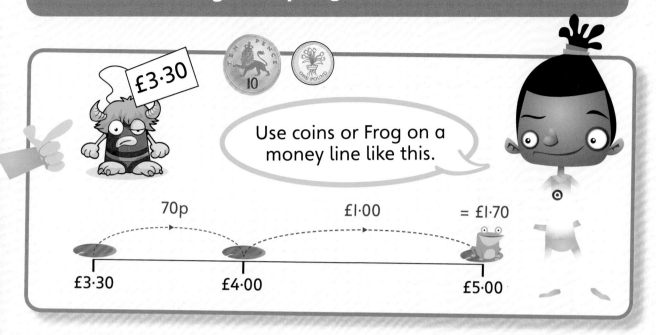

Use coins or Frog on a money line like this.

70p   £1·00   = £1·70

£3·30   £4·00   £5·00

1. £3·80
2. £2·70
3. £0·40
4. £1·40
5. £4·60
6. £3·50
7. £2·20
8. £0·90
9. £4·80

THINK I got £1·30 change when buying a monster with £5. How much was the monster?

● I am confident with subtracting from £5 by
○ counting up.

You pay £5 for each of these toys.
How much change will you get for each one?

1 £3·85

4  £4·45

7  £2·55

2 £1·15

5  £3·65

8 £0·95

3  £2·75

6  £1·95

9 £2·35

A child pays £5 to buy a toy. Write what the toy cost if the change given is:

10 £1·60

12 £4·05

14 £0·85

11 £3·25

13 £2·35

15 £1·45

 **THINK** A toy costs 85p. You buy two of them. How much change do you get from £5?

⬤ ○ ○ **I am confident with subtracting from £5 by counting up.**

44

Look at these problems.

1   How much change?

2 How much change?

Write how much change from £5 for these.

3  £4·20

5  £3·50

7 £2·30

4  You must pay £2·80

6  You must pay £0·60

8  You must pay £1·40

 **THINK** Tom pays £5 for a toy. If he is given £3.70 in change, how much did the toy cost?

 I am confident with subtracting from £5 by counting up.

45

1. Mel buys a magazine costing £3·70. She pays with a £10 note. How much change does she get?

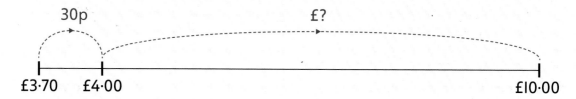

30p   £?

£3·70   £4·00   £10·00

2. Mena has £10 in her money box. She takes out £4·80. How much is left in the money box?

3. Sam has £5·15. He wants to buy a DVD costing £10. How much more money does he need?

4. How much change from £10 would the shopkeeper give to someone buying a bag costing £8·65?

5. Mrs Brown has to pay £7·40 in a car park. She pays with a £10 note. How much change does she get?

6. Simon had £10 when he went shopping. He spent £6·05 of it. How much money does he have left?

 **THINK**   The shopkeeper is given £10. Frog makes the jumps shown in the picture below. How much was the item?

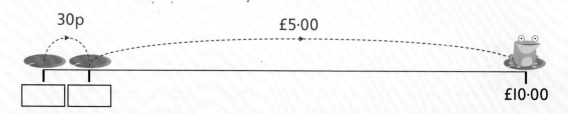

30p   £5·00

£10·00

I am confident with subtracting from £10 by counting up.

Solve these problems using Frog or coins.

1 Shan buys a magazine costing £5·68. He pays with a £10 note. How much change does he get?

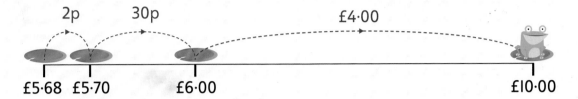

2p	30p		£4·00	

£5·68 £5·70   £6·00   £10·00

2 Amy has £4·18. She wants to buy a DVD costing £10. How much more money does she need?

3 Mr Smith has to pay £3·47 in a car park. He pays with a £10 note. How much change does he get?

4 Joe has a £2 coin, two 20p coins and a 1p coin. How much more money does he need to have £10?

5 Beth had £10 in coins in her pocket. There was a hole in the pocket and she lost £1·69. How much does she have now?

6 Pete bought a £10 pay-as-you-go card and spent £2·37 on calls. How much now remains on the card?

CallTime
PAY-AS-YOU-GO
8848 9929 1163 1956
VALID FROM: 13/07/14
£10·00

7 Shelly has saved £3·20. Ann has saved £4·90. How much more do they have to save to be able to buy a game for £12·50?

8 Jai loves reading. He buys two books for £2·75 each. How much change does he get from £10?

Jim buys a £10 pay-as-you-go card. He has £1·83 left on the card. How much has he spent?

I am confident with subtracting from £10 by counting up.

Place Value of 3-digit numbers

Partition each number and write how many 10s there are.

135 = 100 + 30 + 5

There are three 10s in this number.

1. 573
2. 856
3. 364
4. 817
5. 932

6. How many 3-digit numbers have three 10s? Can you predict? How will you find out?

Now that you think you know, can you prove it?

7. Are there the same number of 3-digit numbers with four 10s? How can you be sure?

8. How many 3-digit numbers have a 0 in the 10s place?

Write how many 100s there are in:

9. 573
10. 856
11. 364
12. 817
13. 932

14. How many 3-digit numbers have three 100s?

 **THINK** How many 3-digit numbers have three 1s?

○ **I am confident with understanding place value of**
○ **3-digit numbers using partitioning.**

Adding two and three numbers

```
    365            300   60    5
  + 129          + 100   20    9
  _____          _____
                   400   80   14
```

 Before doing these additions, predict which will have ten or more 1s and will mean a 10 must be moved.

Use the expanded method shown.

1. 325
    + 246
    _____

2. 623
    + 118
    _____

3. 474
    + 309
    _____

4. 515
    + 367
    _____

5. 467
    + 162
    _____

6. 484
    + 408
    _____

7. 335
    + 259
    _____

8. 558
    + 427
    _____

9. 286
    + 363
    _____

10. 145
    + 783
    _____

11. 367
    + 125
    _____

12. 258
    + 651
    _____

13. 356
    + 627
    _____

14.   33
      23
    + 18
    _____

15.   25
      37
    + 34
    _____

1 537
  + 254

  500 30 7
+ 200 50 4

2 684
  + 174

  600 80 4
+ 100 70 4

3 473
  + 261

6 578
  + 319

9 354
  + 554

4 338
  + 481

7 245
  + 728

10 51
   32
 + 84

5 467
  + 162

8 496
  + 373

11 73
   53
 + 32

 THINK

The answer to this addition is 583.
Copy and complete.

  300 ☐ ☐
+ 200 50 7
  500 ☐ 13

I am confident with adding 2- and 3-digit numbers using the expanded method.

Use the expanded method to answer these additions.

1   216
    + 357

5   386
    + 448

9   289
    + 355

2   448
    + 381

6   576
    + 372

10   352
    + 586

3   478
    + 355

7   358
    + 447

11   447
    + 347

4   468
    + 274

8   386
    + 472

12   378
    + 449

13   35
     26
   + 17

14   38
     27
   + 39

15   62
     73
   + 54

16   81
     94
   + 63

 **THINK**   Can you make this addition work?

```
    2   8
   [ ] [ ]
 +  3   6
   [ ]  1
```

There is more than one answer.

I am confident with adding 2- and 3-digit numbers using the expanded method.

Copy and complete the expanded method to answer these additions.

①

383	300	80	3
+ 454	+ 400	50	4
	700	130	7

③

458	400	50	8
+ 526	+ 500	20	6
		70	14

②

275	200	70	5
+ 673	+ 600	70	3
		140	8

④

239	200	30	9
+ 458	+ 400	50	8
			17

Answer these using the same expanded method.

⑤
```
  584
+ 351
```

⑦
```
  643
+ 349
```

⑨
```
  634
+ 294
```

⑥
```
  847
+ 133
```

⑧
```
  475
+ 482
```

⑩
```
  548
+ 326
```

Now add sets of three numbers using the same method.

⑪

73	70	3
53	50	3
+ 32	+ 30	2

⑫

27	20	7
16	10	6
+ 38	+ 30	8

○ **I am confident with adding 2- and 3-digit numbers**
○ **using the expanded method.**
○

Use the expanded method to answer these additions. Some have been started for you. Copy and complete.

1
```
   375        300   70   5
    54              50   4
 +  33     +        30   3
 ___       _____
                        12
```

2
```
    89              80   9
   353        300   50   3
 +  67     +        60   7
 ___       _____
```

3
```
    75              70   5
    55
 +  36     +
 ___       _____
```

4
```
   248        200   40   8
 + 555     +
 ___       _____
```

5
```
    95
   288
 +  78
 ___
```

6
```
   257
 + 166
 ___
```

7
```
   517
   166
 +  38
 ___
```

8
```
    64
    95
 +  68
 ___
```

9
```
    37
   249
 +  32
 ___
```

10
```
   186
    55
 +  84
 ___
```

11
```
   645
    78
 + 254
 ___
```

12
```
   517
   166
 + 166
 ___
```

THINK For which of these additions would you use a written addition method and which would you do in your head?

352 + 104   352 + 267   352 + 199

I am confident with adding 2- and 3-digit numbers using the expanded method.

For the expanded method you partition each number before adding.

1   859
         68
   +   57
   ———

2   578
        945
    +   59
    ———

3   69
         86
    +   77
    ———

4   697
    + 786
    ———

5   78
        775
    +   96
    ———

6   669
        188
   +   83
   ———

7   979
    + 675
    ———

8   427
        466
    +   89
    ———

9   94
         88
    +   78
    ———

10 857
    + 566
    ———

11   47
        819
    +   22
    ———

12 389
         57
    +   74
    ———

13 593
         68
    + 304
    ———

14 374
        267
    + 266
    ———

15 687
         78
    +   84
    ———

16   87
         94
    +   99
    ———

17   87
        648
    + 186
    ———

18 937
    + 284
    ———

19 637
          9
    + 466
    ———

20 379
        244
    + 375
    ———

I am confident with adding 2- and 3-digit numbers using the expanded method.

Complete these additions.

①
```
    300   60   4
  + 500   70   5
  _____
```

⑥
```
    244
  + 693
  _____
```

⑪
```
    500   70   2
    200   30   5
  + 100   20   8
  _____
```

②
```
    23
    15
  + 36
  _____
```

⑦
```
    300   30   4
          40   3
  + 100    0   8
  _____
```

⑫
```
    482
     75
  + 351
  _____
```

③ 247 + 515 = ☐

⑧
```
    28
    39
  + 15
  _____
```

⑬
```
    74
    82
  + 83
  _____
```

④ 57 + 24 + 16 = ☐

⑨ 123 + 33 + 206 = ☐

⑭
```
    582
  + 388
  _____
```

⑤
```
    37
    23
    54
  + 25
  _____
```

⑩
```
    300   50   4
    200   40   1
  + 300   60   2
  _____
```

⑮
```
    92
    75
  + 52
  _____
```

⑯ Kim runs 641 m and then 287 m more.
How far does she run?

⑰ Karl has £37, Sam has £36 and Lee has £62.
How much do they have altogether?

○● I am confident with adding 2- and 3-digit numbers
○ using the expanded method.

Complete these additions.

1
```
  600   70   3
+ 400   60   5
─────────────
```

6
```
  384
+ 545
──────
```

11
```
  700   90   2
        40   5
+ 100   20   8
─────────────
```

2
```
  33
  82
+ 54
─────
```

7
```
  300   30   4
  200   40   3
+ 100    0   8
─────────────
```

12
```
  482
   75
+ 388
──────
```

3 $36 + 87 + 54 = \square$

8
```
  78
  29
+ 55
─────
```

13
```
  474
  363
+ 112
──────
```

4 $659 + 225 = \square$

9 $41 + 45 + 52 = \square$

14
```
  342
+ 329
──────
```

5
```
  33
  82
+ 51
─────
```

10
```
  500   90   4
        40   3
+ 200   80   1
─────────────
```

15
```
  82
  75
  88
+ 88
─────
```

16 Cho has two bank accounts. In one there is £347 and in the other there is £367. How much does Cho have in total?

17 Amy counts the sweets in three bags. There are 65, 57 and 44 sweets in the bags. How many are there altogether?

○ **I am confident with adding 2- and 3-digit numbers using the expanded method.**

56

Mental addition of 2- and 3-digit numbers

Write out and complete these additions.

1

+	45	92
63		
84		

3

+	76	85
68		
57		

THINK What numbers are missing?

2

+	26	38
47		
59		

+	36	72
		86
53	78	

Answer these additions.

4 534 + 47 = ☐

5 29 + 842 = ☐

6 733 + 58 = ☐

7 918 + 63 = ☐

8 364 + 28 = ☐

9 65 + 726 = ☐

10 367 + 25 = ☐

11 428 + 54 = ☐

12 A pet shop had 47 fish in their fish tanks. A delivery of 75 more fish arrived. How many fish are there now?

13 Mrs Cook measures 528 g of flour into a bowl. She then adds another 57 g of flour. How much flour is there now?

I am confident with adding 2- and 3-digit numbers using a mental method.

Solve these problems.

1 There were 46 men and 17 women sitting in a doctors' surgery. How many people were there altogether?

2 A shop increases the price of a mobile phone by £73. The phone cost £44 before the price rise. What does it cost now?

3 Andy is 82 cm tall. Baz is 27 cm taller than Andy. How tall is Baz?

4 One morning a lorry driver drove 63 km. After lunch he drove 59 km. How far did he drive altogether that day?

5 Choose a bike and a helmet and find the total cost. Do this six times.

THINK Use a calculator to check and mark your own answers.

I am confident with adding 2- and 3-digit numbers using a mental method.

Add these numbers.

1. 456 + 200 = ☐
2. 718 + 30 = ☐
3. 536 + 300 = ☐
4. 316 + 80 = ☐
5. 983 + 6 = ☐
6. 367 + 500 = ☐
7. 523 + 204 = ☐
8. 835 + 22 = ☐
9. 556 + 130 = ☐

10. 645 + 34 = ☐
11. 432 + 305 = ☐
12. 578 + 320 = ☐
13. 674 + 101 = ☐
14. 317 + 199 = ☐
15. 535 + 301 = ☐
16. 262 + 499 = ☐
17. 368 + 401 = ☐
18. 446 + 399 = ☐

Solve these problems.

19. What is the sum of 583 and 205?

20. Find the total of 256 and 340.

21. Add 699 to 135.

 **THINK** James had £445 in a savings account. He pays in more money and now has £547. How much did he pay in?

○ **I am confident with adding 2- and 3-digit numbers using place value and rounding.**

Add these numbers.

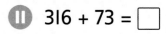
Think about the best way to work out these additions.

1 752 + 200 = ☐

2 463 + 103 = ☐

3 358 + 120 = ☐

4 452 + 49 = ☐

5 837 + 29 = ☐

6 632 + 53 = ☐

7 217 + 502 = ☐

8 322 + 39 = ☐

9 464 + 204 = ☐

10 538 + 150 = ☐

11 316 + 73 = ☐

12 247 + 31 = ☐

13 592 + 305 = ☐

14 812 + 69 = ☐

15 763 + 51 = ☐

16 452 + 107 = ☐

17 329 + 62 = ☐

18 759 + 32 = ☐

19 For which of the questions above did you use rounding to answer?

For which of these questions might you use rounding?

327 + 39   364 + 32   378 + 21   339 + 51

⦿ **I am confident with adding 2- and 3-digit numbers**
○
○ **using place value and rounding.**

Choose the best method to answer each addition.

1. 721 + 104 = ☐

2. 324 + 112 = ☐

3. 432 + 313 = ☐

4. 157 + 602 = ☐

5. 847 + 121 = ☐

6. 663 + 198 = ☐

7. 721 + 143 = ☐

8. 574 + 203 = ☐

9. 752 + 199 = ☐

10. 434 + 298 = ☐

11. 646 + 223 = ☐

12. 375 + 401 = ☐

13. 536 + 340 = ☐

14. 238 + 599 = ☐

15. 573 + 298 = ☐

16. 435 + 113 = ☐

17. 643 + 197 = ☐

18. 364 + 398 = ☐

19. 634 + 132 = ☐

20. 227 + 496 = ☐

Solve these problems.

21. A jar weighs 213 g. It is filled with 354 g of jam. What do the jar and the jam weigh altogether?

22. For her birthday Dita was given £121. She put this together with £398 she had saved already. Does she have enough now to buy a £520 tablet?

I am confident with adding 3-digit numbers using place value and rounding.

written addition of 3-digit numbers

$$\begin{array}{r} 565 \\ + \ 252 \end{array} \longrightarrow$$

| 500 | 60 | 5 |
| 200 | 50 | 2 |

GRAB! Place-value cards

700   110   7   → 700 + 110 + 7 = 817

Complete these using column addition.

1
$$\begin{array}{r} 326 \\ + \ 647 \end{array} \longrightarrow$$

| 300 | 20 | 6 |
| 600 | 40 | 7 |

900   60   13   →

2
$$\begin{array}{r} 438 \\ + \ 534 \end{array} \longrightarrow$$

| 400 | 30 | 8 |
| 500 | 30 | 4 |

→

3
$$\begin{array}{r} 629 \\ + \ 265 \end{array} \longrightarrow$$

| 600 | 20 | 9 |
| 200 | 60 | 5 |

→

4 523 + 239 = ☐

5 476 + 318 = ☐

6 706 + 179 = ☐

7 318 + 478 = ☐

 THINK

| 200 | ☐ | 8 |
| ☐ | 10 | 8 |

800   30   16   → 800 + 30 + 16 = ☐

○
○○○ **I am confident with adding 3-digit numbers using a written method.**

Use an expanded method to add these numbers.

1 326
  + 647

2 145
  + 473

3 453
  + 393

4 255
  + 561

5 464
  + 339

6 415
  + 235

7 522
  + 284

8 633
  + 174

9 726
  + 256

10 458
  + 257

11 366
  + 355

12 287
  + 677

13 A factory makes fireworks. On Monday they made 462 fireworks and on Tuesday they made 375. How many did they make in total?

14 There were 247 adults and 337 children at a firework display. How many people were there altogether?

15 At a firework display, a charity raised £485 from ticket sales and £277 from selling food. How much did it raise in total?

 Write a word problem for the addition 528 + 364.

○ **I am confident with adding 3-digit numbers using a written method.**

63

Investigation

A palindromic number is one which reads the same forwards as it does backwards, for example, 212 and 919.

1. Write two palindromic numbers.

2. Add these using column addition.

3. Underline the 100s and the 1s digit in the answer.

4. Repeat this ten times. Compare the 1s digit and the 100s digit for each answer.

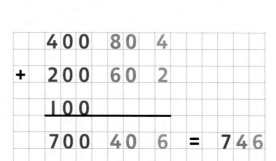

	400	80	4		
+	200	60	2		
	<u>100</u>				
	700	40	6	=	746

5. Which additions have the same 1s and 100s digits? What is special about the two 10s digits for these additions?

6. Which additions have one more in the 100s column than in the 1s column? What is special about the 10s digits for these additions?

7. Can you find pairs of palindromic numbers that have an answer with three identical digits?

THINK Are there any other patterns you can see in the numbers?

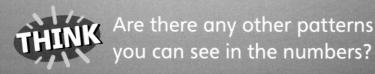

○ **I am confident with adding 3-digit numbers using**
○ **a written method.**

Solve these problems.

1 At a cinema 154 people see the film *Sky* in the afternoon and 227 see it in the evening. How many is this in total?

2 345 adults and 404 children see *Sky* over the weekend. How many is this altogether?

3 In one week at the cinema £563 was spent on popcorn and £514 was spent on drinks. How much is this in total?

4 A salesman drove his car for 326 km on Monday and 457 km on Tuesday. How far did he drive altogether?

5 In a large car park there are 145 empty spaces and 472 spaces that are taken. How many spaces are there in the car park?

6 Jo bought a small second-hand car for £765. She also paid £634 for car insurance. How much did she pay altogether?

7 A vet visited 274 sick animals in January and 299 in February. How many did he visit in total?

8 The vet saw a sick hamster that weighed 426 g. A week later it was 103 g heavier. What did it weigh now?

9 The vet buys some equipment for his surgery. A scanner cost £345 and a computer cost £462. What was the total cost?

THINK Write your own problem for the addition 462 + 357.

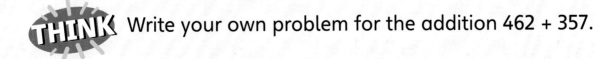

I am confident with choosing a method to add 3-digit numbers.

Telling the time and timing events

Write in words the time on each clock face.

quarter past 4

Write in words the time on each digital clock.

8:30

5:05

3:45

12:15

3:20

9:45

7:25

11:10

10:30

THINK How many quarter past and quarter to times are there between 1 o'clock and 3 o'clock?

I am confident with reading the time to the nearest 5 minutes.

1

5

9

2

6

10

3

7

11

4

8

12

13 Write a time between 6 o'clock and 7 o'clock.

14 Write a time between ten minutes past 2 and a quarter past 2.

15 Write a time between twenty-five minutes past 8 and half past 8.

I am confident with reading the time to the nearest minute.

Write each time in words.

1

2

3

4

5

6

7

8

9

10

11

12

13 Write a time between a quarter past 3 and twenty minutes past 3.

14 Write a time between twenty-five minutes to 5 and twenty minutes to 5.

15 Write a time between ten minutes to 1 and five minutes to 1.

I am confident with reading the time to the nearest minute.

Write the number of seconds for keeping the football in the air.

1. 1 minute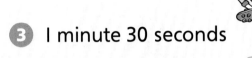

4. 2 minutes 10 seconds

2. 2 minutes

5. 1 minute 15 seconds

3. 1 minute 30 seconds

6. $3\frac{1}{3}$ minutes

Write the number of minutes and seconds for skipping.

80 seconds = 1 minute 20 seconds

9. 120 seconds

12. 72 seconds

7. 90 seconds

10. 150 seconds

13. 130 seconds

8. 100 seconds

11. 85 seconds

14. 145 seconds

THINK You are sponsored 5p per skip. Estimate how many skips you can do in 1 minute. How much will you raise?

15. The first song on my CD plays for 3 minutes 1 second and the second song plays for 2 minutes 55 seconds. How long does it take to play both songs?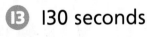

○ **I am confident with the number of seconds in a minute.**

The clock is 5 minutes slow. What is the real time?

①

③

⑤

②

④

⑥

**The alarm is going off in 20 minutes.
What time will each alarm go off?**

⑦
8:30

⑨
7:25

⑪
8:05

⑧
7:15

⑩
8:25

⑫
6:35

THINK It is 8 o'clock. The alarm went off 20 minutes ago. What time did the alarm go off?

○ **I am confident with giving the time 5 or 20 minutes**
○ **later.**

Write each time.

1. 15 minutes later

2. 10 minutes earlier

3. 20 minutes later

4. 25 minutes later

5. 35 minutes later

6. 20 minutes earlier

THINK For questions 1 to 6 write the time 55 minutes later.

Can you see a quick way to add 55 minutes to a time?

Write each digital time.

7. 15 minutes earlier
3:40

8. 10 minutes earlier
4:55

9. 25 minutes earlier
7:45

10. 20 minutes later
7:10

11. 15 minutes later
6:05

12. 40 minutes earlier
3:50

● ○ ○ **I am confident with working out the time a given number of minutes earlier or later.**

1  3:15

4  10:10 DVD

7  9:40 Call List Address Book Settings

2  3:30

5  2:45

8  4:20 COOK 1 2 3

3 12:35

6  formation 7:25

9  10:50

Solve these problems.

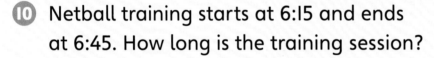

10 Netball training starts at 6:15 and ends at 6:45. How long is the training session?

11 Kel has parked to go shopping. He must go back to his car by 5:40. It is 5:05. How many minutes does he have left?

12 A school has a break from 10:35 to 10:55. How many minutes is the break?

13 A cartoon programme starts at 3:40 and finishes at 4:20. How long does it last?

THINK Emma gets up at 8 o'clock. She takes 15 minutes to eat breakfast, 30 minutes to get herself and her little sister dressed and 10 minutes to get her bag together. If her walk to school takes 10 minutes does she get to school for 9 o'clock?

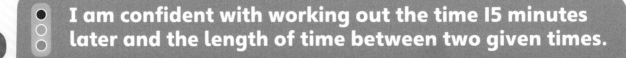

● I am confident with working out the time 15 minutes
○ later and the length of time between two given times.
○

Write the time 15 minutes later as an analogue time.

1  2:45

4  formation 3:55

7  1:40

2  9:25

5  7:50

8  4:10 COOK 1 2 3

3  8:35

6  10:05 DVD

9  9:57 Call List Address Book Settings

Solve these problems.

10 Ed leaves home at 7:55 and gets a bus to school. He arrives at 8:30. How long does it take?

11 Art Club starts at 3:50 and runs until 4:30. How long is Art Club?

12 A school has a lunch break from 12:15 to 1:10. How many minutes is the lunch break?

13 A comedy programme starts at 5:05 and finishes at 5:55. How long does it last?

THINK Chloe and her friends have written a play. It takes 15 minutes to perform. They want to do the play sometime between 12:15 and 1 o'clock. What different start and finish times could they choose?

 I am confident with working out the time 15 minutes later and the length of time between two given times.

Ordering 3-digit numbers

 **672** > **351**

Remember, Croc eats the bigger fish.

Copy the numbers. Write < or > between them to show which is larger.

1. 473   593
2. 148   316
3. 624   298

4. 537   524
5. 856   865
6. 293   291

Write each set of numbers in order, smallest to largest.

7. 351, 287, 615
8. 415, 362, 497
9. 284, 824, 428

10. 356, 154, 373
11. 467, 482, 644
12. 931, 913, 903

THINK Look at the fish numbers for questions 1 to 6. Can you think of a number between each pair?

● **I am confident with ordering 3-digit numbers.**

Write each set of numbers in order, smallest to largest.

1 148, 116, 152

2 417, 482, 467

3 364, 329, 302

4 663, 636, 633

5 396, 354, 372

6 467, 482, 444

7 274, 272, 277

8 980, 908, 911

9 Look at your answers to questions 1 to 8. Write a number between each of the numbers in the set.

There are loads of right answers!

For question 1 you could write the circled numbers:

1 116   (118)   148   (149)   152

 **THINK** Find how many whole numbers lie between:

370 and 380   233 and 243   707 and 717

Write two 3-digit numbers that have 19 whole numbers between them.

I am confident with ordering 3-digit numbers.

1 Use the digits to make different 3-digit numbers.

2 How many different numbers can you make using each digit only once?

There are lots of numbers you can make!

3 Write all the numbers you made in question 2 in order, smallest to largest.

4 Now write a number between each of those that you have written in order.

5 Try this again with these digits:

THINK Using three 1 to 9 number cards how many 3-digit numbers can you make? Is it always the same?

I am confident with ordering 3-digit numbers.

Subtract 2- or 3-digit numbers by counting up

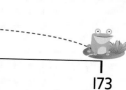

Frog always jumps to the next 10.

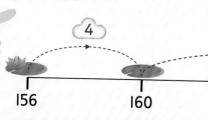

$173 - 156 = 17$

$4 + 13 = 17$

4   13

156   160   173

Use Frog to answer these subtractions.

1 $182 - 148 = \square$

$\square + \square = \square$

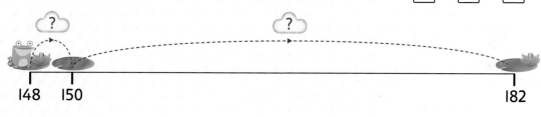

?   ?

148   150   182

2 $155 - 116 = \square$

3 $163 - 127 = \square$

4 $171 - 138 = \square$

5 $144 - 119 = \square$

6 $182 - 145 = \square$

7 $191 - 167 = \square$

8 $164 - 136 = \square$

9 $182 - 157 = \square$

10 $193 - 166 = \square$

11 $121 - 94 = \square$

12 $113 - 88 = \square$

13 $111 - 76 = \square$

THINK

The answer is 35. What numbers could Frog have jumped from and to?

○ **I am confident with subtracting 2- and 3-digit numbers by counting up.**

Use Frog to answer these subtractions.

Remember, Frog always jumps to the next 10.

1. 372 – 318 = ☐
2. 581 – 516 = ☐
3. 473 – 427 = ☐
4. 894 – 846 = ☐
5. 773 – 717 = ☐
6. 661 – 615 = ☐

7. 285 – 227 = ☐
8. 984 – 938 = ☐
9. 381 – 319 = ☐
10. 572 – 515 = ☐
11. 793 – 736 = ☐
12. 883 – 838 = ☐

Use Frog to answer these subtractions.

13. 121 – 68 = ☐
14. 111 – 46 = ☐
15. 123 – 77 = ☐

16. 132 – 57 = ☐
17. 143 – 88 = ☐
18. 134 – 75 = ☐

19. Write pairs of numbers either side of 100 with a difference of 55.

There are loads of pairs!

 **THINK** Frog makes two jumps and ends on 120. The number Frog started at was bigger than 50 and ends in 7. Write some subtractions Frog could be doing.

● I am confident with subtracting 2- and 3-digit
○ numbers by counting up.
○

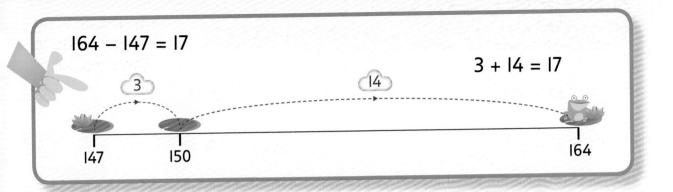

164 − 147 = 17

3 + 14 = 17

147   150   164

Use Frog to answer each subtraction.

1 162 − 138 = ☐

☐ + ☐ = ☐

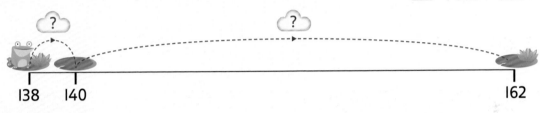

138   140   162

2 166 − 147 = ☐

3 152 − 136 = ☐

4 161 − 138 = ☐

5 144 − 125 = ☐

6 182 − 167 = ☐

7 194 − 166 = ☐

8 242 − 217 = ☐

9 273 − 256 = ☐

10 171 − 144 = ☐

11 283 − 258 = ☐

Frog always jumps
to the next 10.

THINK Frog jumps to the next 10 and then makes a jump of 35 to land on 185. What number did the Frog jump from?

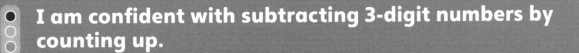

● I am confident with subtracting 3-digit numbers by
counting up.

79

Use Frog to answer each subtraction.

1 283 – 248 = ☐   ☐ + ☐ = ☐

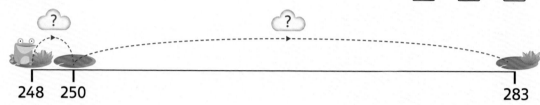

248   250   283

2 155 – 127 = ☐   **7** 384 – 348 = ☐

3 272 – 236 = ☐   **8** 252 – 216 = ☐

4 393 – 367 = ☐   **9** 273 – 235 = ☐

5 164 – 125 = ☐   **10** 481 – 444 = ☐

6 271 – 238 = ☐   **11** 373 – 326 = ☐

Use Frog to answer these.

12 309 – 284 = ☐   6 + 19 = ☐

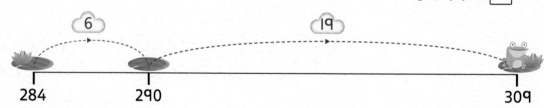

284   290   309

13 403 – 386 = ☐   **14** 311 – 285 = ☐

15 There are 402 pupils in a school. On Monday 377 pupils came to school. How many were away?

16 James had £310 before going shopping. He had £268 when he returned. How much had he spent?

I am confident with subtracting 3-digit numbers by counting up, crossing a hundred.

Use Frog to answer these subtractions.

1. 582 − 528 = ☐
2. 761 − 714 = ☐
3. 472 − 418 = ☐
4. 683 − 627 = ☐
5. 793 − 716 = ☐
6. 892 − 845 = ☐
7. 983 − 936 = ☐
8. 373 − 328 = ☐
9. 285 − 258 = ☐
10. 785 − 717 = ☐

11. 592 − 515 = ☐
12. 493 − 426 = ☐
13. 381 − 318 = ☐
14. 201 − 146 = ☐
15. 513 − 477 = ☐
16. 413 − 388 = ☐
17. 234 − 187 = ☐
18. 421 − 368 = ☐
19. 322 − 267 = ☐
20. 531 − 455 = ☐

Solve these word problems.

21. In the high jump Sally jumps 208 cm and Joel jumps 169 cm. How much higher does Sally jump?

22. There are 412 parents in the hall to see the school play. 356 of them are women. How many are men?

23. Nisha has £278. She wants to buy a phone that costs £311. How much more money does she need?

● I am confident with subtracting 3-digit numbers by
○ counting up, crossing a hundred.

Solve these problems.

1

2

3 Sam had £273. He bought a tablet for £238. How much money does he have now?

4 In July a sunflower was 156 cm tall. By September it was 194 cm tall. By how much had it grown?

5 One young elephant weighs 271 kg and another weighs 238 kg. How much heavier is one than the other?

6 There are 365 cars parked on level 1 of a car park and 328 cars parked on level 2. How many more cars are on level 1 than level 2?

7 There are 477 people at a rugby match. If 428 of them are adults, how many are children?

8 An airline pilot flies 385 miles on Monday and 326 miles on Tuesday. How much further did he fly on Monday than Tuesday?

 Make up your own story for 472 – 417 and answer it.

Mental subtraction methods

Answer these subtractions.

Choose a method such as counting up (Frog), counting back or rounding for each question.

1. 347 – 21 = ☐
2. 286 – 39 = ☐
3. 152 – 127 = ☐
4. 351 – 318 = ☐
5. 674 – 49 = ☐
6. 188 – 51 = ☐
7. 367 – 14 = ☐
8. 265 – 238 = ☐

9. 632 – 16 = ☐
10. 132 – 85 = ☐
11. 564 – 528 = ☐
12. 772 – 15 = ☐
13. 275 – 29 = ☐
14. 471 – 51 = ☐
15. 582 – 21 = ☐
16. 381 – 338 = ☐

True or false?

17. The answer to 108 – 56 is 45.

18. Subtracting a multiple of 10 does not change the 1s digit.

19. It is impossible to subtract a number ending in 9 from a number ending in 1.

If the statement is false, how could it be changed to make it true?

 Make up one true and one false statement about subtraction.

○ **I am confident with choosing a mental method of subtraction.**

Doubling and halving

Answer these doubling and halving problems.

1. What is half of 24p?

2. $46 \div 2 = \square$

3. What is half of 82p?

4. Halve 68.

5. Split 74 cm in half.

6. Share 38p between two.

7. Halve 56.

8. Half of 72 is $\square$.

9. $94 \div 2 = \square$

10. Half of 36 is $\square$.

11. Divide £92 by 2.

12. $78 \div 2 = \square$

13. For a school sports day, 42 oranges are cut into half. How many halves are there?

14. The children in each class were put into two equal teams. Class A has 28 children. How many in each team?

15. An 86 cm piece of ribbon is cut equally in two and each is tied to the winner's trophy. How long is each piece of ribbon?

16. Mr Shar gives £96 to his two sons, Akmal and Raj, to share equally. How much did each son get?

17. Akmal and Raj decide to give £29 each to a charity. How much did they give altogether?

18. The boys now have £38 altogether. How much is that each?

- ● I am confident with doubling and halving numbers
- ○ up to 100.
- ○

Answer these doubling and halving problems.

1. $56 \div 2 = \square$

2. What is half of 38p?

3. Split 76 cm in half.

4. Double 54.

5. What is half of 72p?

6. Double 312.

7. Double 124 is $\square$.

8. Halve 168.

9. Multiply £72 by 2.

10. $\square \div 2 = 46$

11. Half of $\square$ is 58.

12. $146 \div 2 = \square$

13. The 52 playing cards in a pack are put into two equal piles. How many cards are there in each pile?

14. Mandy and Andy are dealt 16 playing cards each. How many of the 52 cards are not dealt to them?

15. Sara plays 'Patience'. She has 17 cards in her hand and twice as many on the table. Are any of the 52 cards on the floor? If so, how many?

16. Ali and Ellie agree to combine their earnings. Ali gets paid £28 for cleaning a car, and Ellie gets £34 for babysitting. If they add their money together then share it, how much do they have each?

17. Half the number of people in a train carriage are adults and half of the adults are women. If there are 28 women, how many people are in the carriage altogether?

Multiply using the grid method

Mrs Lee is taking her 5 sons on holiday. Work out how much she would pay for the items shown. Use the grid method.

GRAB! Place-value cards or coins

£23 £13 £16 £18 £24

 3 × 24 = 72

×	20	4	
3	60	12	= 72

1

 4 × 13 = ☐

×	10	3
4		

2

3

4

5

6

7

THINK What is the easiest way of working out the 13 times-table up to 10 × 13? Talk to a partner about how to do this and see how far you can get!

I am confident with multiplying numbers between 10 and 25 by 3, 4 and 5 using the grid method.

Use the grid method to answer these.

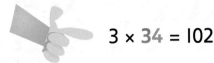
$3 \times 34 = 102$

×	30	4	
3	90	12	= 102

1 $5 \times 23 = \square$

×	20	3	
5			= $\square$

2 $17 \times 3 = \square$

3 $26 \times 5 = \square$

4 $19 \times 4 = \square$

5 $3 \times 26 = \square$

6 $32 \times 4 = \square$

7 $33 \times 5 = \square$

8 $3 \times 28 = \square$

9 $27 \times 4 = \square$

10 $5 \times 34 = \square$

11 $29 \times 4 = \square$

THINK   This grid is partly done and the answer is worked out. There are two ways of making it work. Can you find both of them?

×		5	
			= 175

$3 \times 14 = 42$

3×10

3×4

30

12   $= 30 + 12 = 42$

×	10	4	
3	30	12	= 42

Use a grid to answer each multiplication.

1 $5 \times 14 = \square$

×	10	4	
5	50	20	= $\square$

2 $15 \times 3 = \square$

×	10	5	
3			= $\square$

3 $5 \times 16 = \square$

×	10	6	
5			= $\square$

4 $16 \times 4 = \square$

5 $3 \times 17 = \square$

6 $19 \times 4 = \square$

7 $18 \times 3 = \square$

 **THINK**   Multiply 13 by 3. Multiply 14 by 3. Then multiply 15 by 3. Look at the answers. Explain what you notice.

●
● **I am confident with multiplying numbers between**
● **10 and 25 by 3, 4 and 5 using the grid method.**

Use the grid method to answer these.

$3 \times 17 = 51$

×	10	7	
3	30	21	= 51

3×10 3×7

30   21   = 30 + 21 = 51

1 $5 \times 23 = \square$

×	20	3
5			= $\square$

2 $32 \times 4 = \square$

×	30	2
4			= $\square$

3 $27 \times 3 = \square$ **6** $3 \times 29 = \square$

4 $5 \times 24 = \square$ **7** $5 \times 27 = \square$

5 $26 \times 4 = \square$ **8** $28 \times 4 = \square$

 **THINK** If the answer to $\square \times \square\,\square$ is an odd number, what do we know about the numbers in each of the boxes? Can we say for definite that any of the box digits are odd or even?

● I am confident with multiplying numbers between
10 and 30 by 3, 4 and 5 using the grid method.

89

Use the grid method to answer these multiplications.

$4 \times 36 = 144$

×	30	6
4	120	24

= 144

1 $5 \times 28 = \square$

×	20	8
5		

= $\square$

2 $37 \times 3 = \square$

3 $4 \times 34 = \square$

4 $42 \times 5 = \square$

5 $3 \times 44 = \square$

6 $28 \times 4 = \square$

7 $36 \times 5 = \square$

8 $38 \times 3 = \square$

9 $4 \times 29 = \square$

10 $43 \times 4 = \square$

11 $5 \times 37 = \square$

12 $38 \times 4 = \square$

13 $45 \times 5 = \square$

THINK Multiply 13 by 4. Now multiply 26 by 4. Look at the two numbers. Can you explain what you notice? Repeat to find answers to 14×6 and 28×6.

● I am confident with multiplying numbers between
10 and 45 by 3, 4 and 5 using the grid method.

Use a grid to answer each multiplication.

$3 \times 39 = 117$

×	30	9
3	90	27

= 117

1 $28 \times 4 = \square$

×	20	8
4		

= $\square$

2 $37 \times 4 = \square$

3 $3 \times 36 = \square$

4 $23 \times 5 = \square$

5 $4 \times 32 = \square$

6 $3 \times 43 = \square$

7 $37 \times 5 = \square$

8 $4 \times 44 = \square$

9 $5 \times 42 = \square$

10 A tin of mushy peas costs 17p. How much for 4 tins?

11 Cherry tomatoes weigh 14g each. How much do 5 of them weigh?

12 Peaches come in packs of 4. How many peaches are there in 19 packs?

13 A lorry delivers 3 crates of cola. There are 24 bottles in each crate. How many bottles are there?

 **THINK** Which is more? 3×43 or 4×34

I am confident with multiplying numbers between 10 and 45 by 3, 4 and 5 using the grid method.

$3 \times 42 = 126$

×	40	2	
3	120	6	= 126

1 52 × 4 = ☐

2 3 × 46 = ☐

3 48 × 5 = ☐

4 4 × 47 = ☐

5 3 × 53 = ☐

6 56 × 5 = ☐

7 4 × 58 = ☐

8 3 × 59 = ☐

9 In each bag there are 42 sweets. How many in 4 bags?

10 A tin of sweetcorn costs 34p. How much is 3 tins?

11 Five children each have £44. How much money in total?

12 How many legs do 53 sheep have?

13 Jack is charged 5p a minute for phone-calls. How much does he pay for 32 minutes?

14 Three chicks in a nest each weigh 44 g. If the nest weighs 50 g, what is the total weight of the nest and chicks?

☐ × ☐☐ = 180

What would the second number in this question be if the first number was 3? or 4? or 5?

● I am confident with multiplying numbers between
10 and 60 by 3, 4 and 5 using the grid method.

92

Practising calculations

Use mental methods to answer these.

1. $\square \times 8 = 56$

2. $8 \times \square = 48$

3. $64 \rightarrow$ double $\rightarrow$ double

4. What is half of 82p?

5. $94 \div 2 = \square$

6. $463 + 103 = \square$

7. Halve 68.

8. Half of 36 is $\square$.

9. $\frac{3}{4}$ of $8 = \square$

10. $\frac{3}{5}$ of $10 = \square$

11. How much change from £10 if you spend £3·80?

12. $352 + 49 = \square$

Use the column method to find the totals.

13.
```
   75
   55
+  36
────
```

14.
```
  517
  166
+  38
────
```

15.
```
  645
   78
+ 254
────
```

16.
```
  517
  342
+ 329
────
```

Use Frog, counting back or rounding to answer these.

17. $155 - 116 = \square$

18. $182 - 157 = \square$

19. $347 - 21 = \square$

20. $152 - 127 = \square$

21. $164 - 136 = \square$

22. $632 - 16 = \square$

Use the grid method for these multiplications.

23. $27 \times 3 = \square$

24. $4 \times 34 = \square$

25. $3 \times 29 = \square$

26. $5 \times 38 = \square$

Number puzzles

Five children sit in a ring and count in equal steps. Jon always starts with zero.

If they count in 3s, who says:

1 12? **2** 21? **3** 15? **4** 27?

If they count in 4s, who says:

5 8? **6** 16? **7** 32? **8** 44?

9 When they count in 3s are the numbers they say odd or even? Write what you notice.

10 When they count in 4s what do you notice?

11 Jon starts with different numbers for four more rounds and they count on in 10s. Copy and complete this table to show the first five numbers they say each round.

Jon	Kim	Bo	Ben	Tom
26	36			
78				
158				
426				

12 Add more rows to your table with your own starting numbers.

sorting machine

This is a sorting machine.

If you put 25 into the machine and follow the route to box A you get the number 350.

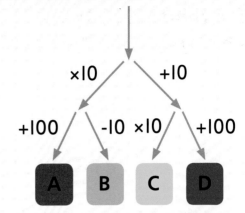

25 × 10 = 250

250 + 100 = 350

What number do you get if you put in 25 and go to:

① Box B?

② Box C?

③ Box D?

You could draw a table.

④ Choose other 2- or 3-digit numbers to put into the machine and work out what numbers will reach each box.

Investigate this:

⑤ Use digits 1 to 9 to make three 3-digit numbers. You may only use each digit once. Write them in order and draw a loop around the middle number.

| 3 | 2 | 9 | 5 | 6 | 1 | 7 | 5 | 8 |

⑥ Do this as many different ways as you can.

⑦ Find out if it is possible for the middle number to be:

198   321   517   941   831

Explain your thinking.

Series Editor
Ruth Merttens

Author Team
Jennie Kerwin and Hilda Merttens

Published by Pearson Education Limited, Edinburgh Gate, Harlow, Essex, CM20 2JE.

www.pearsonschools.co.uk

Additional contributions by Hilary Koll and Steve Mills, CME projects Ltd.

First published 2013

16 15
10 9 8 7 6

British Library Cataloguing in Publication Data
A catalogue record for this book is available from the British Library

ISBN 978 1 408 27848 2

Printed in Slovakia by Neografia

Acknowledgements
We would like to thank the staff and pupils at North Kidlington Primary School, Haydon Wick Primary School, Swindon, St Mary's Catholic Primary School, Bodmin, St Andrew's C of E Primary & Nursery School, Sutton-in-Ashfield, Saint James' C of E Primary School, Southampton and Harborne Primary School, Birmingham, for their invaluable help in the development and trialling of this book.

Every effort has been made to contact copyright holders of material reproduced in this book. Any omissions will be rectified in subsequent printings if notice is given to the publishers.